Poetry o.. ...
Picket Line

Edited by Grim Chip
& Mike Quille

with a Foreword by
Phill Jupitus

The philosophers have only interpreted the world, in various ways.
The point, however, is to change it
—Karl Marx

First published 2018 by Culture Matters.
Culture Matters Co-Operative Ltd. promotes a socialist
and progressive approach to art, culture and politics. We run
a website which publishes creative and critical material on politics and
culture; manage Bread and Roses arts awards; deliver cultural education
workshops to trade unionists; publish books; and contribute to the
development of culture policy in the labour movement.
See www.culturematters.org.uk

Foreword

by Phill Jupitus

I have always thought there's an unrecognised grace and beauty in a picket line. Also, they are a huge embarrassment to the organisations being picketed. The fact that, for centuries, news organisations have portrayed the objectives of those who stand on them as avaricious, unreasonable or somehow evil is a testament to the strength of the image. A picket line is the simplest, most direct manifestation of the will of people to be treated with some measure of fairness. Ordinary workers, forced to stand outside a place of work, because they simply won't take shit any more.

The *Poetry on the Picket Line* crew have been pitching up at many and various sites of industrial action, and showing their support with impromptu alfresco performances, for a few years now and the scope of their activities has grown over that time. This collection encompasses the passion, empathy, wit and commitment of their work.

It is not merely the job of art to hold a mirror up to society from a distance, the best of it needs to engage with hearts and minds on the ground. *Poetry on the Picket Line* is a perfect manifestation of this. It's odd to say that I wish there was no need for them. But the fact is that over the coming years they're going to be getting busier if anything. So thank you for buying this book, and supporting them and their work, and by extension, everybody out on the line.

Don't cross them.

Acknowledgements

Culture Matters and Poetry on the Picket Line would like to thank the following union organisations for sponsoring the publication of this book, so that more money from sales can be donated to union strike funds:

PCS
(particularly the Culture Sector group)

RMT
(particularly the London Transport Region)

TUC London, East and South East
(particularly the Culture and Leisure Industries Committee)

Contents

Poetry on the Picket Line and the National Gallery

by Candy Udwin, PCS National Gallery branch

In 2015 PCS members at the National Gallery spent 111 days on strike. We were fighting against privatisation, against victimisation and also against policies intent on turning our museums and galleries into party venues for the rich, rather than places where everyone has a chance to be inspired by the creativity of human beings.

On 111 picket lines we learnt that solidarity is alive and well, and that if you ask, you will get support from all around. Thousands supported us and raised over £160,000 for our strike fund. We discovered not far below the surface, the political mood of anger against austerity and desire for an alternative that was about to catapult Jeremy Corbyn to the leadership of the Labour Party.

On 111 picket lines and protests and demonstrations we discovered that enjoying and producing art linked to our fightback made us stronger. We had exhibitions and artists' days on the picket line. We asked different unions and campaigns to organise a solidarity day picking their favourite painting from the Gallery. Our sunflower banner, after van Gogh, spread to t-shirts. We hand-painted 1,000 sunflowers for May Day.

And we had poets! People who were brave enough to come and share their poems on our picket lines. Poets who added some different words to the hundreds of speeches. Words to wake people up, to make them think, to make them laugh, to make them realise they might like poetry.

We are grateful to those poets who were part of the movement that kept our strike going. And proud that Poetry on the Picket Line was born out of our struggle.

Poetry on the Picket Line are following an old art, but developing a new tradition of using art as a weapon, fighting to defend what we have and for a better world, where everyone has a chance to explore and enjoy our creativity.

Every picket line should have one.

Poetry on the Picket Line, The National Gallery Campaign and Show Culture Some Love

by Clara Paillard, President of PCS Culture Group

Show Culture Some Love was born from the seeds of the National Gallery
campaign.
PCS union forging alliances with other Trade Unions
Community, Disability, Black campaigners
Came together

In the midst of some much brutality,
After 5 years of austerity,
Security, invasion of galleries
Police called to the picket line,
We needed some love

Show Culture Some Love grew up from the creativity of workers determined
to stay.

Workers, raise your paintings!
Workers, broaden your arising!

We are Show Culture Some Love,
We are an alliance of Trade Unions and friends,
We are cultural workers, we are cultural lovers, we are cultural creators.

We are Show Culture Some Love,
We show solidarity,
Art as a weapon,
Culture as a Human Right
After three conferences, workshops, debates, discussions,
Workers and non-workers arise from the music sheet,
Gallery assistants curate their own exhibitions,
Cinema workers brandish a paint brush

They all write and murmur words of wisdom, poetry that says...
Show Culture Some Love
And take over from bosses and politicians.
Show Culture Some Love, we said
And they looked at us, puzzled, baffled, afraid.

Don't be afraid, we said, all we want is...
Show Culture Some Love.

8

The Show Culture Some Love campaign was launched in March 2015 at a conference organised by the CLIC (Creative and Leisure Industries Committee) of the Southern and Eastern Region of the TUC (SERTUC). It builds on the PCS union Culture Group anti-privatisation campaign at the National Gallery and involved other unions in the art and culture sector: BECTU, Musicians' Union, Equity, TSSA and UCU, as well as visual and performance artists, academics, students, supporters of arts and culture as well as campaign groups such as Disabled People Against Cuts (DPAC), Black Activists Rising Against Cuts (BARAC) or Art Not Oil.

We have held three events in London, took part in the national demo for Libraries, supported numerous trade union campaigns, produced a disobedient exhibition, held protests and lobbies to support art and culture as human rights. We are now building the movement in the Regions and Nations.

Our main aims are to campaign for an end to the cuts in arts and culture budgets caused by the pro-austerity policies of the current government and to make the case for greater investment in the sector. Access to art and culture is not only a human right but can also help tackle racism and discrimination, improve health, and contribute positively to the economy. As a result of our efforts, a number of the Show Culture Some Love demands were integrated in Jeremy Corbyn's arts policy.

Show Culture Some Love also exists to help promote solidarity and publicise campaigns in the culture sector.

Time to end austerity in arts & culture!

showculturesomelove.wordpress.com
Facebook: /showculturelove
Twitter: @showculturelove

Poetry on the Picket Line and the Picturehouse

by Obi Saiq, Picturehouse striker

For almost two years now, we the workers across several Picturehouse cinemas have been in dispute with our bosses, Picturehouse Cinemas, who are owned by multinational cinema giant, Cineworld. Our main demands have been: to be paid a London Living Wage (Currently set at 10.20, at present Picturehouse pay 9.37); to have access to company sick pay & maternity pay; recognition of our chosen union BECTU (except The Ritzy, Brixton, which already has recognition agreement).

The origins and timeline of our dispute lay in the summer of 2014. Back then workers at the Ritzy, Brixton, were being paid just barely above the minimum wage. The workers got together that summer and launched a series of strikes & walkouts that culminated with the company sitting down & agreeing to boost their wages by 26% and most importantly, a "commitment" from management to become a living wage employer within two years.

Two years passed, union reps at the Ritzy approached Picturehouse management about progress with the Living Wage. Management bluntly told the workers they had no intention of paying the Living Wage. It was clear their "commitment" two years ago was a stalling tactic. In response, the workers from the Ritzy began striking in the Autumn alongside workers at Hackney Picturehouse who had also begun organising a while ago and were ready to fight. Over the space of 6 months, 3 other sites joined us (Central, East Dulwich, and Crouch End). We started 2016 with 80 union members across all sites, now we're at almost 300.

Our dispute has certainly had an effect on the company, many film festivals have pulled out, many creatives don't want to be associated with this company and have called them out publicly. The tide is in our favour, Picturehouse can either negotiate now & salvage their reputation or continue their hard headedness till its too late for them. Either way we will win. The workers of these cinemas are getting organised.

Poetry on the Picket Line have been great supporters of ours, providing moral support with their presence, entertainment with their poetry, and material support via fundraising they do from gigs. They are super lovely and their support is much appreciated. The labour movement needs to exert its presence on all aspects of society including entertainment. Poetry on the Picket Line is an example of that, we should do our best to promote socialist entertainers and performers who in turn promote socialism into the wider consciousness.

Picket Lines are Poetry

by Paul Salgado, Union Organiser, United Voices of the World

To walk out on strike is a big decision for any worker to take, and you can imagine such a decision would be even more difficult for precarious and marginalised migrant workers—abused, threatened and slandered by bosses and the press—to take.

But the migrant workers organised in our United Voices of the World independent union have got a bit of a reputation for winning lately, as we've taken down Harrod's, the LSE, City law firms and City banks, proving that collective direct action is the best medicine to take to deal with poverty pay, inequality and abusive bosses.

And no little part of this collective fightback involves having fun while shutting down the workplace. This is where Poetry on the Picket Line comes in, keeping spirits high, and putting smiles on workers' faces, whilst punching the boss in the face.

What the picket line poets deliver are not only rapier-like stanzas and verses that make the bosses cower, but solidarity, respect and appreciation for the workers taking a stand.

While some strikers respond with incredulity to hear poetry on their picket line, everyone appreciates the support for their fight. Not everyone can be a poet, but all of us can strike. And when the day comes when millions of workers begin to take their own future in their own hands, you can bet that Poetry on the Picket Line will be standing on the barricades giving us a soundtrack to the resistance.

Poetry on the Picket Line

Matt Abbott

The Wall

The Refugee Community Kitchen:
daily since December, seven days a week.
Over half a million cooked meals,
over half a million tonnes of food;
twenty-four/seven,
through volunteers and donations.
The United Kingdom government:
Seventeen million pounds
on a thirteen-foot wall.
According to immigration minister,
Robert Goodwill (yes, Goodwill):
"People are still getting through.
We have done the fence,
now we are doing the wall."
As I walked through the Jungle on 6 August,
I found a dozen people on a handmade building site.
They'd dug the foundations,
and with wooden planks,
they're constructing the frame of a gym.
There's already a boxing venue
and a theatre.
If you walked through Dover on 30 January,
you'd see flags saying, "refugees not welcome",
as well as knuckle dusters, knives and hammers.
A demonstration led
by Britain First and the National Front.
They clashed with anti-fascists,
and the police tore in with riot gear;
all, of course,
at the taxpayers' expense.
Just like the fence, just like the wall,
just like the guns, and just like the bombs.

Tories Out

We find solitary shoes on beaches from
a dinghy that's capsized. Millions flee
from Western bombs and we all act surprised.
Meanwhile on Fleet Street,
Corbyn rocks the yacht.
A movement swells, but still they yell:
"the Trots have lost the plot!"
Thatcher said she weren't for turning;
May makes me dizzy. Hammond hails
stability, but he's no better, is he?
The brunt of Hunt in wings and wards
wide across the land,
whilst Johnson wears buffoonery
to mask his Bullingdon brand.
In safe seats, complacency is starting to erode.
Neglect that spreads between the blinks
like potholes in the road.
Deprive us of attention,
seduce us in campaigns;
as soon as that rosette's removed,
you tighten up the chains.
When Sophy Ridge makes Auntie Beeb
resemble Rosa Luxembourg, and LBC
make bourgeoisie of fascists without a job.
Osborne's at the *Evening Standard*,
the *Metro*'s owned by the *Mail*.
The Sun still blinds; keeps shining on
with vitriolic tales.
Scores of children left to starve;
reduced to weary wisps.
Surviving through the Food Bank
or a multipack of crisps. Left sleeping
in a hospital on two chairs placed together.
A desperate parent's pay day loan;
pushed far beyond their tether.
This is not about one leader.
It's the fight of a generation.
Millions reaching breaking point
through ruthless degradation.
It's a fight against austerity where
the "with" rule the "without",
so let's come together, day by day...

...and kick the Tories OUT!

Janine Booth

Sides

Just before the Sun raises its head above the parapet
One side of the sky is light, the other horizon dark

We stand by a tree whose trunk has a carpet of decorous lichen on one side
The other side plain and furrowed with bare and turreted bark

The road was deserted for most of the night, but now that the traffic is starting
The middle of the highway is no longer a safe place to stand

So take to the pavement alongside the fence which is tall and robust and so narrow
That even the neighbourhood cats cannot sit there and must choose a side where they la

There's no amber on pedestrian crossings, there's only red or green
So you have to cross or not cross, there's nothing in between

Come to the gate where we stand in a line
With armbands and coffee and 'official picket' sign

This isn't multi-faceted, this is no polygon
This line has only two sides—which one are you on?

The Eleventh Commandment

I'd rather go to prison or be given a huge fine
Or have cosmetic surgery from Doctor Frankenstein
Sit through a boring lecture on interior design
Yes, I'd rather do most anything than cross a picket line

I'd sooner scratch my itches with a prickly porcupine
Or spend the night in darkest woods when evil stars align
De-skin my legs with sandpaper and wade through lakes of brine
Yes, I'd rather drown in vats of rats than cross a picket line

I'd rather drink a cocktail made of sweat and turpentine
Or live beneath a spiky hedge in Lower Lichtenstein
Lie face down in the middle of an open-cast coal mine
Yes, I'd rather eat stale camels' feet than cross a picket line

I'd rather be like Tarzan and go swinging from a vine
Or dive off that big bridge and then go swimming in the Tyne
Bathe naked with piranhas in the Hyde Park Serpentine
Yes, I'd rather lose my other eye than cross a picket line

I'd rather rub a massive turd and try to make it shine
Or dip some poo in superglue and stick it to my spine
Invest my lot in Enron stock and watch its sharp decline
Yes, I'd rather go to Hell and back than cross a picket line

I'd rather face the rising storm in 1939
Or have my photo taken standing by a TURN RIGHT sign
Pretend to have the time of day for Michael Heseltine
Yes, I'd rather have my nails pulled out than cross a picket line

I'd rather take a solemn pledge to never drink more wine
Or place my genitalia in the mouth of a dead swine
Become a Shadow Minister, then run off and resign
Yes, I'd rather scrape the barrel's arse than cross a picket line

I'd rather turn my bedroom to a Justin Bieber shrine
Or use an Off-Peak Travelcard at twenty-five past nine
Send Iain Duncan Smith a secret, scented Valentine
But I'd never, no not ever, ever cross a picket line

Grim Chip

A Higher Education

There's no lack of grit,
Or of determination,
On these picket lines.
They've made it in—
Or rather out—
Despite the conditions.
It's the terms that are the issue.
No going back until they get
What they're entitled to,
What they have earned.
It's a study in itself, this.
You get to keep
What you're prepared
To make a stand and fight for.
A higher education
And a lesson learned.

Ice Age

(when the entire continent of Europe was covered by a gigantic glacier,
and there were no borders)

As if cutting off your nose to spite your face
Was successful cosmetic surgery,
'The people of Britain have spoken'.
Democracy. Inaction.
The body politic broken.
Bullshit, bluster and downright lies,
It's no surprise when the disenfranchised
Stick two fingers up to the establishment.
Who knows what they meant?
Who ruined race relations?
Who blamed immigration?
Who supped with the devil
They knew was in the detail?
It's an epic fail to understand
Whose dick it is in your arse.
When it's the ruling class.
The whole damn thing was a farce.
Listen, let me articulate this clearly,
Understand I mean it most sincerely...

I don't want to take my country back,
I want to take it forward.

Owen Collins

Royal London

Dedicated to the staff and patients of the Royal London Hospital

The wind carries a turquoise sticker across the picket line,
And on the same breeze comes car horns,
Truck horns, bike bells and bus horns,
Hooted, tooted shows of support.

It's cold, and I can't feel my toes,
Or my fingers. But I can feel... Something else.

The turquoise sticker is still swirling in the slipstream,
Dancing in the updraft.
Signs are made.
Placards are raised to the rumbling grey Whitechapel skies.
The rain shall not fall. Not today.

GUM registrars, anaesthetists and GPs huddle together,
Junior Doctors and their patients stand together.
Banners are hung up. Pastries are passed round,
And high above, outside the deep blue mosaic windows,
The turquoise sticker is still floating,

Carried by a wind
Which wafts and drifts round the Royal London,
Which is blowing and transmitting the support
That is still sounding, from scooters, cyclists and cement mixers.
They're behind you.

The wind is behind you.
It's blowing in your direction.
A change is coming. Victory is coming.
It's in the air.

We Stand With You

We stand with you.
And those of us who can't stand
Will sit with you,
And lie with you,
Until you can make them stand
Which you can,
And you will,
And when you do,
We stand with you.

You've got our backs.
And our ribs and our skulls,
Our tarsals and our carpals,
Our kidneys and our lungs,
Our hearts and our minds.
We entrust ourselves to you,
So entrust yourself to us.
You've got our backs,
And we stand with you.
We're in your hands.
And in your minds,
We're in every detail of expert precision,
We're in every case of free provision,
We are in the dedication you provide,
In the acres of knowledge for which you strive
For years and years.
You make us strong,
You keep us safe,
You save our lives,
And all the time,
We're in your hands,
You've got our backs,
So we stand with you.

You're on our case.
And on our wards and on our streets
And on our wavelengths and our beats,
And we are on your side,
And on your picket line today,
And we will stand up, proud to say,
That we are with you all the way.

You're on our case,
We're in your hands,
You've got our backs
And we've got yours too,
And we will stand with you.

Mark Coverdale

A Manifesto of Sorts

It starts
Eat sleep
Jam tarts
It's about hearts
Not football
It's the arts
Of dodging
Through
The shit
And calling out
What it
Is it
Means to us
As we get the bus
An' give up seats
For the needier
Sail our trawlers
Catch the media
And throw it back
From whence
It came
'Cos on the
Gallery wall
We're all in
The frame
So take aim
With words
Of benefaction
Give dancing
Lessons to
Rival factions
Off yer arses
Stick hard hats on
For the writing's
On the wall
It's a call for
Finger extraction
It's time for
What they
Really hate
And what they
Really hate is
Action

Timber!

I like trees.

You can sit
under them
and write
about them.

The bosses
are like trees,
we sit under them
and write about them.

I like chainsaws.

Nadia Drews

And so the Struggle

Speeches clapped
And then shut up
In thumbed fist,
Wrinkled skins of books
With slogan spines,
Backs broken,
Crooked.
And so the struggle.

Marches passed
Like channels changed
On blurred screens,
Dated placards wave,
Forced forward,
Steps stride,
Out of range.
And so the struggle.

Meetings held,
Missed quotes in mind,
Hands raised,
Breaths count,
Loss left behind,
Dimmed vision
Now newly defined.
And so the struggle.

Not Entitled

You are not entitled,
Your claim has been suspended,
You did not attend,
You were informed,
You do not qualify,
You did not submit,
You did not declare,
You are not entitled.

You are not entitled,
Your mother wore curlers in the street,
Your claim has been suspended,
You did not attend,
Your dad was redundant,
You were informed,
You did not submit,
You were seen bending down,
You did not declare.

If you want to appeal
You can seek advice,
A decision has been made.
You are not entitled.

You *can* seek further advice.

Fran Isherwood

If in Doubt, Use a Motto

Don't insult a crocodile until you've arrived safely on the other bank —
Zulu proverb

Do insult the sharks that operate the banks but
give them the wrong phone number.
Sometimes pointlessness is the whole point.
Don't try to convert a pigeon to your religion
unless you are really bored.
Cut down on refined flour. Let bagels be bygones.
Cease your addiction to Doctor Who. Let Zygons be bygones.
Don't count your chickens before they've got out of The Hatchback.
A stitch in thyme is a waste of herbs and thread.
You will only resent time spent on bureaucracy
If you don't write a poem first.
Look after yourself. Lead the Grim Reaper a right merry dance.
Look before you sleep. Don't use a horsey torso as a bed.
Don't hoover with a horse's hooves. You won't see him for dust.
Be a political animal even if it is a poodle.
Sometimes you need to go out just so you can come in again.
Don't lend your stilts to a chicken. She will rule the roofs.
Get your ears tested. The ferry crossing may not
be working but it is not due to Paul Weller.

Safe as Houses

Blitz. Lightning ruptures indigo sky
Tumult of rain pelts torpid tin roof
Row of saplings, puny branches
Mexican Waving not drowning ...
Yet. Breakers recklessly
wreak wreckery upon and
no -regretfully happy-slap.
clodhoppers of slimestone.

Devoured from underneath
Cliff crumbles, gives in,
bows his aged head.
His toupee of sodden dune grass
slithers. Caravan lurches drunkenly
on precipice, stuttering and wheezing,
about to jump.... Then,
remembers he forgot his fags.

Inside, last night's empties party on
Dodgems rollick, spewing out fag ends.
Perspiration races down faces
of lace-petticoated window panes.
Signals: gunmetal, nails-on-blackboard gull shrieks
that could awaken the dead. Yet not
the inebriated, stewing in their own gases,
ensconced in grubby, blue, quilted cocoons.

Hokusai vision halted. Dawn. Fresh.
Calm, blue sky smiles upon early bird dog walker.
Warblers serenade man and enthusiastic beast.
A rumble. Geoff checks sky for signs of thunder.
Behind him, a downwardly mobile home plunges.
"They're a long time", thinks Barbara,
"Not thunder again!" She wraps dressing gown
tighter to keep out the chill. Puts kettle on.

Michelle Madsen

Passports

This year we start at the end.
Ordnance map, wet screen. Continents missed by sightless eyes.
All borders invisible. Trust you to spot one.

On the train,
Your chest falls in time with the torn shirt of the man across the aisle.
Four eyes at rest. two hearts beating, two unstilled chests.
A man, another man,
Tapping out a shoeless tattoo on the side car of the train.
Both babes. Slack lipped and sticky eyed,
Cradled in stained blue velour arms.
Twins in a buggy which pays no regard to skin tone, birth or bank balance.

Journeys like these don't require passports
But faith of feet, leaping blind.
Our journey demanded a passport but no one came to check.

In my burgundy book I collect stamps
Like my brother collected football stickers.
My 2010-2016 escape annual.
I'd like to say where I want to go without a currency of nationality
But my voice deserts me and the night rises like the 6 am sky in June,
Except it's January, and the sky is red.
And this new year is just as old as the one before it.
Born knowing. A gum-cracking, side-walk spitting nappy
holster rifle-toting
Infant warrior of a year
Wear it. Crash diet it, squeeze it into razor sharp suits
Future proof it before it learns the word guilt.
Hang it to dry. A sacrifice to our ills.
Our last indulgence.

Not in my Ballot Box

When did you last see the leaves turn?
Watch green leach to yellow in the wind?
Vote for life, mark the holes in the path.
The seasons change. Sometimes we don't see it.
The deserts bloom, glaciers melt or freeze.
The earth turns, regardless.

Regardless the earth turns, blind to the tar
grubbing its lungs or apes switching tools for
limbs, busy with the business of eliminating.
I watch the leaves crisp.
Their veins burst in exhaustion, hurtling to an end.
One day empathy will flow

easily for trees. We'll lay memorials to the mess
On the path, plastic candles keep vigil
till batteries die, illuminating notes pinned to melting bodies.
After the leaves go,
we quiz the bare branches, asking
how they will cover their nakedness.
They are empty now. Regardless
the world turns. When will it be
spring again, we wonder?
We bombed the trees, their
sap stains the street. They hid our
enemies. Nameless, faceless.

Glued to screens, we wonder how this came to be.
Cold metal kisses the needles of the Christmas tree,
tickles hope's frozen toes.
I heard that this year the escapees asked for
lessons from Houdini. How to unpick a lock.
Hold your breath underwater. Disappear.

I heard they got lace underwear,
well-meaning thongs,
the odd sock.
I hear others coming now
Precision whining
tipped for an unknown target.

Eyeless travellers blast through borders
We never asked for them
to come, but let them.
They don't knock.

The Repeat Beat Poet

For Us, Being Angry is Hereditary

In British summertime you'll catch me daydreaming,
Looking for a New England,
On a search for a Black Mecca,
Theorising about Atlantis,
Or imagining any place better.
What I want from the world right now are better stories,
Ones where inequality isn't furthered by Tories,
Or where daily news doesn't rely on the same sensationalist stories,
The glorification of the gory,
Wilfully misinforming the public every morning
As we flick between the terrifying, the confusing, and the boring.

I'd like a tale where Trump doesn't prevail.
Where what you put in your body doesn't land you in jail,
Where state policy doesn't endanger and deport the frail,
And wealth isn't concentrated at one extreme of the social scale.

Where is it written in stone that our current system cannot fail?

To the authors, and self-appointed directors, of our current reality,
Take your academic expertise, your coded speech and legalese,
And use it to do something that keeps education accessible at least!
Stop the rise of university tuition fees,
Or the closing down of libraries?
You can't escape the irony that you learnt what you know,
Ergo how to oppress me, mostly for free.
Add to that fact you could get a house for cheap,
Using your heavily subsidised education,
You've decided to damn a generation with already high stress,
And increased powers of communication,
To extortionately high rents and age-based wage discrimination,

Way to bet against the future of your nation...

All of which is basically to say,
If you're a young person right now,
And want to improve yourself,
Or look after your health,
You better already have some assets, some power, some wealth.

Otherwise this system will kill you in stealth.

There's Going to be Uproar

This microphone's a baton,
This poem's a machine,
These similes are weapons
If you know what I mean,

This comparison's essential,
Similarity sublime,
Never just coincidental
And it's true because it rhymes

This rhyme is overrated,
While still being enough,
To uplift a sunken soul
When the seas are rising rough

This narrative is cliché
Predictable and cheap,
This criticism is blasé,
Throw it on the trash heap,

These verses are linear,
Circular and reflexive,
Lines intertwined
With a flow so inventive,

With intended breaks.
To emphasise impact
Using literature to heal
Like a syntax stimpack,

Bringing back life to stagnant waters,
This poem revolutionises sons and daughters,
Mothers, fathers, rich and poor,
All can sense the change in store

Because now the voices are building up.

Before long, more will wake up.

Each head primed and ready,

To break down doors.

To shout! To ERUPT!.

Listen closely...

David Turner

S—for Sugar

I don't remember any coffee shops
on Lupus Street in the mid-eighties
—at that age I probably assumed
everyone, like my nan, drank instant
from the saucer (in front of three-bar
gas fires) chair legs sinking/rooting
themselves in lino or armchairs
consumed on one side by knitting
patterns, cushions stained Consulate
yellow (Ebury Bridge to Pimlico
School contained everything she
needed) at that age I took for granted
that if we turned left out of The
Avenue   we'd   end   up   on
Buckingham   Palace   Road...   we
always turned right (Max Bygraves
((smile of the Sunday lunchtime
drinker)) leers at us from glossy LP
covers) before they filled in the end
of Peabody Avenue the terraces and
Plane Trees perfectly framed the
ruin of Battersea Power Station and
the wasteland of Nine Elms behind—
we now long for the ridiculous idea
that those chimneys might house a
theme park.

Taxis on Old Pye Street

I stand—profile toward the wind hoping to mimic your breath on my neck.
    Cars throw their lights. Ignored, they shatter on wet concrete.

        Bleed out over tarmac.

As south of the river, clouds are pulled to earth. Sucked into the Heygate's
exposed foundations.

    The memory of your brittle, cold fingers, still pressed into my
    palm, lingers and I dwell on grinding those digits to dust.

  This beauty is a menace.

  I (vaguely) recall telling you that an x-ray of my uncle's shoulder
  looked like a crushed bag of crisps.
                                You didn't flinch.

    We talk of destroying each other.

Bus windows—blank canvasses. Fur-lined parka hoods etch fine-lines into
condensation. Hearts and arrows traced by fingertips. (Initials.)

Lizzy Turner

And What's in Yours?

What frightens me is
I can't see exactly
what's stuck on the inside of my body,
what, alongside coffee staining,
bad thought never quite sloughed,
curdling on a raw wall,
what might interrupt my
blood at a later date,
something sitting in there,
a gristle rock,
no memory of mine
but with its own,
haunted little misery of a thing,

I'm scared to think
inside of my body,
feel from the surface
quiet bumps which don't
reveal the features underneath,
what event made my
waist bend in like this?
pulled me together and
where did it go?
I think of how the
things get in and get
transported through the system,

I fear the poisons which
won't leave the body fully,
clawmarks in the padding
round the exits, scars
of substance, abuse of the
flesh by the brain,
what damage, what consequences,
what strange becoming of my body
while I sleep?

Schiele Would Have Loved You

You are oblivious as a portrait
when you're standing at the centre of the gallery,
your face is bowed to your notebook,
right leg trailing to the side in that way my art can't stretch to.

It is not for you to know how you look
when you are still, and all the other people
circulating like planets,
while you're awakening even the deceased artists,
who reach out from their paintings to claim you.

How love comes to you,
as the colours of the sea come to your expression
as the best of the light comes to your face
when you lift it to the skylight,
beyond which something has called you under its instruction—

I have to capture you quickly in this position.

You turn at last to look at me
and your smile is jewels which cut me
with the liquid of their brightness,
in that way my words can't reach.

Tim Wells

Here in Sunshine or in Shadow

An Irish paraffin
sings 'Danny Boy'
to the
Show Culture Some Love
trade union pickets.
We join in.
It's the all of us.
We have
no money,
no power.
We do have culture.
It's the all of us.
They've slapped
a price on it.
But they can't buy it.

There's No Smoke Without...

Richest borough in the country.
There's no smoke without...

We're all in it together.
There's no smoke without...

Services cut because "Get stuffed!"
There's no smoke without...

They can't even look us in the face.
There's no smoke without...

They fiddle while.
There's no smoke without...

Anger is building up.
There's no smoke without...

Poets' Pen Portraits

Matt Abbott is a spoken word artist and activist from Wakefield. After starting out with short sets on the indie music scene in late 2006, a Love Music Hate Racism event in April 2007 saw his poetry and political activism align for the first time. Over the last few years, he's shared a stage with names including Paul Weller, The Fall, Sleaford Mods, Jeremy Corbyn, Ken Loach and Sara Pascoe. Matt runs spoken word record label Nymphs & Thugs, is the Poet-in-Residence at the National Coal Mining Museum for England, and is an ambassador for Trinity Homeless Projects and Eureka! The National Children's Museum. His show, *Two Little Ducks*, explores the core reasons behind the working-class Leave vote, whilst recounting his experiences at the Calais Jungle either side of the referendum.

Janine Booth is a Marxist motormouth who is in the second half of her poetry adventure having ranted in the 1980s and recomposed in 2014. She writes and performs poems funny and serious, formal and random. Janine's poems have been published in numerous mags and anthologies, and in four of her own little books. Check out her website: www.janinebooth.com

Grim Chip is not the man you hoped to meet. An active trade unionist, he writes poetry in his spare time and prefers picket lines to literary salons when it comes to sharing his work.

Owen Collins is a Witney-based poet who believes in socialism, love at first sight, and not having to pay to use the toilet at major railway termini. He has acted as support poet for both Madness and a member of the House of Lords, and his poetry has been taught in schools from Chichester to Hamburg. He finds all of this as unlikely as you do.

Mark Coverdale is an Art School Mod Poet. Born in Darlington the year Elvis died. Now in London via Oldham writing and performing socially and politically observational poetry.

Nadia Drews was born in San Francisco and brought up in Greater Manchester. A Socialist mother with a suitcase of vinyl recordings by Leadbelly and Howlin' Wolf led her to revolutionary politics and, eventually, to write and perform songs about changing the world. The stories of working-class lives in the songs grew into plays and she left Manchester having written and co-produced *I Love Vinegar Vera (What Becomes of the Brokenhearted)*. Now living closer to family roots in the East End of London she began to perform poetry and found the voice she was looking for.

Fran Isherwood is a poet with a comedic bent (bit like Housemaid's Knee) who gads about on the London poetry circuit and (sometimes back of) beyond and co-hosts a monthly gig. Her poems lurk in several anthologies, print and online periodicals and in *Poems in the Waiting Room* which was distributed in surgeries and hospitals. Her pamphlet, *Swimming with Endorphins*, was published in 2015 and longlisted in the Saboteur Awards. Originally from Manchester, she has previous form as a singer, comedy improviser and actor.

Michelle Madsen is a poet, theatre maker and investigative journalist. She has performed on four continents and is a regular at Glastonbury, Latitude and the Edinburgh Festival. She is the host and creator of (possibly) the world's only poetry panel game, *I'm Sorry I Haven't Haiku*. She's the host and founder of Bargerella, a floating all-female vaudeville show and also makes guerila, campaigning theatre. She was shortlisted for the Poetry Rivals award, has been published in numerous titles including Rising and her debut collection, *Alternative Beach Sports*, is published by Burning Eye Books.

Peter deGraft-Johnson is **The Repeat Beat Poet**, a London-based poet and emcee who fuses stream-of-consciousness writing and Hip Hop culture to capture and extend moments of time, thought, and feeling. He has performed at the Royal Albert Hall, the Edinburgh Fringe, represented the University of East London at UniSlam, and is a Nozslam Champion. Peter also regularly produces and hosts the monthly spoken word events Boomerang, and PenTing. His debut poetry show, *D.O.W.N*, debuts in October 2018.

David Turner is the founding editor of the Lunar Poetry Podcasts series, has a City & Guilds certificate in Bench Joinery (along with the accompanying scars), is known to the Southwark Community Mental Health Team as a service user, and has represented Norway in snow sculpting competitions. Originally from London but now living in Bristol. Widely unpublished. Working class.

Lizzy Turner is a poet attempting to relocate from London to Bristol with the Cockney poet she fell in love with. She spends most of the day standing at an espresso machine, and she co-edits the Lunar Poetry Podcast. Lizzy recently launched new poetry podcast 'a poem a week', as a companion to Lunar Poetry Podcasts.

Tim Wells is made of reggae, lager top, pie and mash, and Leyton Orient FC.

Publications

Recent publications from Culture Matters, available from http://www. culturematters.org.uk/index.php/shop-support/our-publications

arise! by Paul Summers

This pamphlet-length poem celebrates the rich heritage and culture of mining communities, which is expressed so vibrantly and colourfully in the marches, the banners, the music and the speeches at the Durham Miners' Gala. It invokes the collective and co-operative spirit of past generations of men and women who worked and struggled so hard to survive, to build their union, and to organise politically to fight for a better world.

Arise! also celebrates the new, resurgent spirit in the Labour Party, led by Jeremy Corbyn, and the renewal of support for socialist solutions to the country's growing economic and social problems.

It's wonderful to see the proud history of the Durham Miners' Gala represented in this powerful poem. Paul Summers has managed to capture the spirit of the Miners' Gala and its central place in our movement's mission to achieve 'victory for the many, and not the few'.

—**Jeremy Corbyn**, leader of the Labour Party

10% of the proceeds of sales of this book will go to the Durham Miners' Association Redhills Appeal, to help turn Redhills into a cultural hub for the area.

The Combination by Peter Raynard

Peter Raynard has written a remarkable new long poem to mark the 200th anniversary of Marx's birth, and the 170th anniversary of the publication of the Communist Manifesto.

Like the Manifesto, it protests the injustice and exploitation which is integral to capitalism, and the growing gap between capitalism's productive potential and the unequal distribution of its benefits. And like that Manifesto, it is a dynamic and powerful piece of writing—pungent, oppositional and unsettling.

This poetic coupling is something else. It's a re-appropriation, a reclamation, a making sing. It's bolshie (yes, in every sense), provocative and poignant too. It takes the Manifesto back from all that is dead, dry and terminally obfuscated. It's a reminder of reality, the flesh on the theory. It gives Marx to those of us who need him most. Not just relevant, but urgent. Not just angry, but hopeful.
—**Fran Lock**

The Things Our Hands Once Stood For by Martin Hayes

Martin Hayes is the only British poet who writes consistently and seriously about work, and about the insanity of a society where employees are seen merely as mere 'hands' to be employed and to make money for their employer.

Work is what most of us have to do, and the workplace is where most of us spend a large part of our lives. Work should be about creatively transforming the world around us to meet all our needs, but it isn't. For the many, work is hard, precarious, poorly paid, unsatisfying and alienating, and constantly threatened by automation. Workers 'never get to share in its profits/but always seem to get to share/in its losses'. Why? Because of the few who own their labour 'squeezing away at people's lives like they were plastic cups'.

The clear message of his poetry is that those who do the work should own, control, and benefit fully from it. They should, in the last words of the last poem, 'start the revolution that will change everything', and show that 'all of our fingertips combined/might just be the fingertips/that keep us and this Universe/stitched together'.

A Third Colour by Alan Dunnett and Alix Emery

Through the sheen of vivid, simple narratives and vignettes, we glimpse more disturbing, ambivalent themes of alienation, dislocation and suffering, the psychological fallout of anxiety in modern capitalist culture.

A Third Colour is a book of visionary, poetic parables and dystopian, uneasy images. It is a principled and skilful expression of, and protest against, the world we live in.

Muses and Bruises by Fran Lock and Steev Burgess

Fran Lock's socialist poetry weaves psychological insight and social awareness into themes of poverty, mental health problems, sexual abuse, domestic violence and political struggle. It is vivid, lavish and punchy, combining a deep sense of anger and injustice with vulnerable empathy and compassion.

The fragmented yet coherent collages of Steev Burgess complement and enhance those meanings perfectly. His images dance with the poems, singing together about muses and bruises, fantasy and reality—grind and grime with a lick of glitter.

Bring the Rising Home! by Mike Jenkins and Gustavius Payne

Weaving through both poems and images are themes of individual isolation and alienation, and the urgent need to recognize that collective action is necessary to change the conditions of working people. Mike Jenkins's vivid, lyrical poems work together with Gustavius Payne's bold, striking, and deeply sympathetic paintings, complementing each other perfectly.

Here is a poetic and painterly union of two socialist Welsh artists who, in their own brilliant, artistic way, are interpreting and changing the world—bringing the Rising home!

On Fighting On! The Bread and Roses Poetry Anthology 2017

An anthology of poems from the Bread and Roses Poetry Award 2017, sponsored by Unite.

We sponsored the first Bread and Roses Poetry Award because we believe that our members, and working people generally, have an equal right to join in and enjoy all the arts, and other cultural activities. We believe we should be able to afford them, get to them, and enjoy them, and that art should seek to engage with all sections of the community. Working-class people face a continual cultural struggle to defend our cultural commons, to keep cultural activities open to the many, not the few.

—**Len McCluskey**, General Secretary of Unite